Emotional Unavailability & Neediness:

Two Sides of the Same Coin

Gabriella Kortsch, Ph.D.

Rewiring the Soul

"*Rewiring the Soul* is a revelation of insight into the foundations of human suffering and transcendence. It not only lays out the essential steps for inner freedom and joy but it also illuminates the way to true human potential: the stunning and dynamic "Possible Self." Written with clarity, compassion and wisdom, this chronicle is not one of mere speculation, but arises from the depths of hard won personal experience. Gabriella Kortsch is a spiritual master for our time."
Paul Rademacher, Executive Director, The Monroe Institute; author of *A Spiritual Hitchhiker's Guide to the Universe*

"Gabriella Kortsch uses her talent and experience to write the instruction manual on rewiring the soul. An in-depth guide on life, love, spiritual evolution and our integration within the universe."
Michael Habernig & April Hannah; Producers of *The Path: The Afterlife* and The Path 11 Documentaries

"This meticulously researched and crafted book is clearly the masterwork of a profoundly gifted healer of the soul, one who thinks deeply, feels deeply, and cares deeply about the well-being of the world and its humankind. Reading it will change your life; beginning to live actively any of its ideas, principles, and suggestions will *transform* your life. And bring you safely and joyfully home to your true self, your soul. I found it dazzling, challenging, and wondrously useful."
Peggy Rubin, Director, Center for Sacred Theatre, Ashland, Oregon; author of *To Be and How To Be, Transforming Your Life Through Sacred Theatre*

"*Rewiring the Soul* is a thoughtful guide to the peace and joy that self-government through inner awareness brings. In the words of author Gabriella Kortsch, anyone's ideal 'possible human' becomes their actual reality by following the simple inner steps in this remarkable book."
Jim Wawro; author of *Ask Your Inner Voice*

"*Rewiring the Soul* is the human being's directory to the soul. This inspirational book asks you to simply open yourself to the possibility that you are much more than you have considered yourself to be; in truth, you are spirit in form living a soul-directed life. It is a breakthrough for those seeking practical assistance, those of a more mystical bent, and every soul awaiting discovery. Read it cover to cover first; then place it close at hand to pick up every time your mind strays from your soul's message radiating from within the heart."
Toni Petrinovich, Ph.D.; author of *The Call: Awakening the Angelic Human*

"I thought I could pick just one chapter to write a review, but I couldn't …. I was glued to the chair as I read *Rewiring the Soul* … a literary, in-depth masterpiece to the human psyche, behavior and ultimate transformation. Exquisitely written, beautifully executed."
Ali Rodriguez, Business Coach, co-author of *Mastering the Art of Success* with Jack Canfield and Mark Victor Hansen

"*Rewiring the Soul* is one the best introductions to the spiritual life I've ever read. Not esoteric but real-world and practical. Read it and Soul is no longer just a dogma, nor hypothesis, it is made real and as much a part of your being as your toes. We usually shut off our inner voice, yet by recognizing this aspect of ourselves we begin to discover our essential nature, our intuitive truth, and that becomes our loving guide. The author illustrates the limitations of living only as the mind's Ego, and demonstrates in practical terms how we can transcend this by awakening a conscious viewpoint, following the path of our intuition and feelings, no longer separated from our body and the reality around us, and integrating at last our Soul's inner guidance and wellspring of love. The implications are profound."
Peter Shepherd; Founder, TransForMind; author of *Daring To Be Yourself*

"A glance at the contents of *Rewiring the Soul* will tell you much about the values promoted: *awareness, freedom, peace and love*. I fully agree with the author that it is all about re-connecting with our authentic 'loving self': it is only then that we can deeply

transform our life while also inspiring a transformation in the lives of others! Through this powerful book, Gabriella Kortsch *honestly* shares her love of serving the inner potential and the spiritual growth of human beings with passion, joy and commitment."
Elisabetta Franzoso; International Speaker, Coach, author of *Stella's Mum Gets Her Groove Back: A True Story*

"The Soul doesn't get sick but it does need nourishment; if not it seems as if our life starves to death. This wonderful book by Dr. Gabriella Kortsch is definitely healthy "Soul food". It becomes clear that as the personality endeavors to "rewire" the Soul, it is its own energy or conscious awareness that is elevated to that higher level where the invisible becomes visible and experienced as peace, joy, love and freedom. A treat to enjoy and celebrate."
Eric Rolf; author of *Soul Medicine: The Heart of Healing*

"This book is a gift to humanity, a valuable tool in aiding seekers to accomplish mastery of their own lives. Gabriella Kortsch provides clear steps to help people find peace in a practical and powerful way. She does not ask you to give up anything other than what no longer serves you. Brilliantly written!"
Hillary Raimo; Author & Radio Host

The Tao of Spiritual Partnership

"All humans seek the illusive touch of another's Soul, which opens us to the sense of belonging to something bigger than the self. Dr. Kortsch has given us the true "tao" of relationship in this brilliant exploration of emotional tapestry. Through her wise teaching, we can not only discover ourselves in the reflection of our partners, but we can learn how to access a *spiritual* connection that sets us free. We will be grateful for this illumination of spiritual partnership for generations to come. Thank You, Gabriella."
Chris Griscom: Spiritual Leader, Author of *Ecstasy is a New Frequency & Time Is an Illusion*

"In my years of researching life plans and soul contracts, I've learned that we plan (before we're born) to have romantic relationships for the purposes of healing and expansion. And this is just what Gabriella Kortsch so eloquently and comprehensively shows you in *The Tao of Spiritual Partnership*: how your primary love relationship may be a sacred vessel that transports you and your partner to a place of mutual healing and expansion."
Robert Schwartz: Author of *Your Soul's Gift: The Healing Power of the Life You Planned Before You Were Born*

"Gabriella Kortsch has a rich international background with unmatched experience in her field. *The Tao of Spiritual Partnership* is a unique blend of wit and wisdom; she encourages us to take responsibility for our relationships, while recognizing and seizing the opportunities for our own personal spiritual growth."
William Buhlman, Author of *Adventures Beyond the Body*

"*The Tao of Spiritual Partnership* is an excellent, smart guide to making your relationships blossom. Your partner will thank you for buying this book! Why struggle with relationships when you can have a fulfilling spiritual partnership? Dr. Gabriella Kortsch's newest book *The Tao of Spiritual Partnership* deftly shows the way to satisfying interactions with the loves of your life."
Jim Wawro, Author of *Awakening Counsel: A Practical Guide to Creating the Life You Want to Live.*

"Riveting.The importance of fulfillment of a life well-lived through understanding and practicing self-love is paramount and candidly expressed in this one-of-a-kind book. I have gained deeper insights into my own life, and the promise of the book: "to love without needing" is profoundly delivered!"
Ali R. Rodriguez: Business Coach Strategist, Co-Author of *Mastering the Art of Success*

The Power of Your Heart: Loving the Self

"In *The Power of Your Heart,* Dr. Kortsch takes the well known self-help axiom of "first, one must love oneself, before one can love others" and proceeds to deliver nothing less than a profound and authentic way of living and being that heals the soul and improves one's interactions and relationships with others. By clearly distinguishing her love-based concept of self-love from the fear-based concepts of narcissism, egotism, and neediness, Dr. Kortsch provides a step by step guide that, if honestly applied, puts one on a life's path of peace, satisfaction, contentment, and happiness."
Thomas Campbell; author of *My Big TOE*

"From childhood we are taught to mercilessly nitpick our essential being in pursuit of a mythical perfection. With deep insight and impeccable clarity, Dr. Gabriella Kortsch, Ph.D., turns the tables to illuminate the liberation possible when loving ourselves unconditionally. In so doing, she provides a road map to undiscovered bliss and wholeness. A must-read for anyone on the path to self-understanding!"
Paul Rademacher, Author of *A Spiritual Hitchhiker's Guide to the Universe: Travel Tips for the Spiritually Perplexed,* CEO of Lucid Greening, Editor of *Inner Story Magazine*

"This book explains the vital importance of loving yourself and why that is not in the least bit selfish. If there is a lot of love inside you, then you have more to share, in fact, it becomes a bottomless well. With love in your heart, your choices will be based on understanding, compassion and empathy. An inspiring read!"
Peter Shepherd; Founder, TransForMind; author of *Daring To Be Yourself*

"*The Power of Your Heart* is a book to satisfy the soul's hunger and deserves to be read by every adult, parent, teacher and adolescent. It assures us that it is not just permissible, but essential, to love ourselves, undoing the conditioning that has kept us in a state of unworthiness and self-doubt, and sets us on the path to emotional, psychological, and spiritual growth. Love of self is a prerequisite to

love of others and love is the foundation on which we are building a new world of compassion, joy and good will."
Linda Stitt; Author of *Acting My Age*

In the art of loving the self, this book takes the phrase 'self help' to the next level. Gabriella Kortsch has made the case and built the foundation that ultimately will become your own self-empowering path to true happiness and prosperity. Using real world situations along with quotes from the masters scattered throughout the book, you will soon discover the power of your own heart and make it a habit of loving the self.
Michael Habernig & April Hannah; Producers of *The Path: Afterlife* **&** *The Path: Beyond the Physical*

Also by Gabriella Kortsch, Ph.D.

Books:

Rewiring the Soul: How Your Connection to Yourself Can Make All the Difference

The Tao of Spiritual Partnership: Background Music in Daily Life That Can Enhance Your Growth

The Power of Your Heart: Loving the Self

4-Hour Audio CD Programs

Relationships:
Priceless Tools for Self-Understanding, Growth, and Inner Freedom

Fatherless Women and Motherless Men:
The Influence of Absent Parents on Adult Relationships

Coming Soon (A Novel)

The Master Calls a Butterfly

Emotional Unavailability & Neediness: Two Sides of the Same Coin

Gabriella Kortsch, Ph.D.

Cover Design by Ignacio Martel

Library of Congress Cataloging-in-Publication Data

Kortsch, Gabriella

Emotional Unavailability & Neediness: Two Sides of the Same Coin / Gabriella Kortsch.

Includes biographical references

ISBN-13: 978 – 1500913458

ISBN-10: 1500913456

1. Intimacy (Psychology) 2. Self-love 3. Love 4. Happiness 5. Wisdom 6. Mental Healing I. Kortsch, Gabriella II. Title

2014915121

First Edition

I do not love you except because I love you;
I go from loving to not loving you,
From waiting to not waiting for you
My heart moves from cold to fire.

I love you only because it's you the one I love;
I hate you deeply, and hating you
Bend to you, and the measure of my changing love for you
Is that I do not see you but love you blindly.

Maybe January light will consume
My heart with its cruel
Ray, stealing my key to true calm.

In this part of the story I am the one who
Dies, the only one, and I will die of love because I love you,
Because I love you, Love, in fire and blood.

Pablo Neruda

Contents

Foreword

Much - although by no means all - of the material contained in this book has appeared in print throughout portions of my previous books, as well as in my monthly newsletter articles and daily blog posts, all written between 2006 and 2014. Parts of it have also appeared on my radio shows that were broadcast over a period of seven years between 2004 and 2011, as well as in my workshops in the *Conscious Journey Within* Series. My intention had never been to utilize this material until just recently when I realized how little of it is available under one roof, so to speak, for those who want a comprehensive look at what is such a prevalent issue in the lives of so many individuals.

The actual insight for me that this material has not been readily available came during one of my weekly *Live Your Best Life* discussion groups that I have been holding since the beginning of 2010. The topic that day had been of a different nature, but members of the group asked several questions that segued into emotional unavailability and neediness. They then requested that we discuss that topic instead of the one that had originally been on that day's agenda.

And so I spoke at length about emotional unavailability and neediness. You could have heard a pin drop, not because I am so eloquent, but rather, because it is a subject that affects so very many - whether from one end of the spectrum (emotional unavailability) - or the other end (neediness). And of course, because those two diametrically opposed points of the spectrum often manifest in one single individual, where one side may come to life in one relationship, and the other side in another over the course of a lifetime, and the patterns often merge indiscernibly from one relationship to another until the person affected by them comes to greater awareness, I recognized that some of the material already in existence, and interwoven with new material, could be brought together between the covers of one book, as said, and thus be made available for those who could benefit from it.

****

This syndrome, that plays such havoc with people's lives, does not however, necessarily sentence them to a lifetime of bad relationships. Both the emotionally unavailable person and the needy one can come to understand what has brought them to this place in their lives and with that understanding, can begin to change, ultimately living a life of much greater emotional freedom.

Nevertheless, in my practice I have observed that those individuals who lean more to neediness than to emotional unavailability appear to find it somewhat less difficult to grow and develop in a healthier direction. They seem to have slightly greater ease in understanding exactly what it is that keeps them in that role and pattern, and therefore are able to move more readily towards a healthier relationship paradigm. I speculate that this is the case because by leaning towards the neediness end of the spectrum, they are less afraid - overall - than those individuals who lean towards the emotional unavailability end of the spectrum, and who fear emotional *vulnerability* with all their being. The defense mechanisms of the latter group were also set in motion when they were very small children and have grown increasingly strong and automatic indeed. For a good part of their lives they may have little - if any - awareness about this at all. And so, if they come to therapy and are made to realize *why* they behave as they do in relationships, they may most certainly recognize themselves (information, after all, can be so freeing), and even - on occasion - find that information of great interest. But they will not always - nor so easily - choose to do something about that fear of vulnerability that keeps them in this emotional strait jacket of their own making.

Having said that, as you will come to see in the pages of this book, it *is* possible to grow beyond emotional unavailability. It *is* possible to come out from the other side of this painful pattern in your relationships. The clients (both male and female) I have had the honor to work with that had lived a portion of their lives under the shadow of emotional unavailability and who had the valor to deal with it consciously and with the intention of changing it because they recognized that their relationship would never have a decent chance at being healthy unless they did this, demonstrated to me over and over again that it *is* possible. But to do so requires courage, persistence, and the desire and intention to do this for yourself, your inner well-being and your inner freedom.

We will delve in great detail into numerous concepts in subsequent chapters of this book that will help you understand how to resolve emotional unavailability and neediness in your life, but there are some basic things that need to be stated now.

As with much that relates to inner growth and inner freedom producing work, being conscious and aware is a hugely crucial element in the equation. Without it, little will change - at least not by choice. And it is precisely this element of choice that arises once you have gained awareness of yourself and once you have become conscious of so much that occurs in your daily life that you will be able to tap into the potential emotional freedom that such choice offers you.

Yet the daily practice (not so much implying time-consuming, specific, or onerous exercises, as much as the daily *practice* of remaining *aware*) required in order to become conscious and aware and the brutal honesty that will necessarily ensue if you are choosing to properly apply this brilliant lens of awareness to yourself and all that you think, feel, say, and do, as well as to all of your reactions, are the two main reasons why many give up. Some find the daily practice too tiresome, boring, or simply don't believe in it, others keep *forgetting* to do it (which is *also* a choice), others yet simply believe they are already aware, and so they muddle on in dark rooms of their inner world where nothing changes regarding the twin issues of emotional unavailability and neediness. And the second aspect with respect to the courage required to look at the self with such brutal honesty, scares many off. We are not accustomed to applying such a strong microscope to the self and it can be daunting.

Nevertheless, as said, I have seen many do it successfully and with great valor. None of it is necessarily too difficult; it is simply a question of having the intention to carry it off and then applying the information presented in this book to your own life.

You may be anxious to get right to it - to start making those changes that will help you and your life move forward, and that will allow you to disentangle yourself from the iron shackles of this double syndrome. While I encourage you to read the entire book in the 'correct' order, I know that I frequently err in this regard myself when I begin a new book, impatient to get to the heart of the matter, and so if you feel you want to go there first, read Chapter 14 and read about the eleven steps that will show you how to reach your goal. However, you will be more successful if you first make time to read all the other chapters before you actually take on the task of shifting your current parameters.

One final point: in our emotional lives we tend to attract to us - and have relationships with - people who have attained (or stagnated at) the *same* level of emotional maturity as we have. Emotional maturity is not the same as emotional intelligence, although they are related. Think of it like this: imagine a woman - Nina - who has worked on her emotional self for quite some time. Perhaps she was married, had children, and is now in her late 30's or early 40's, divorced, well-situated professionally, and ready to move into a new relationship. Perhaps she was needy or emotionally unavailable, and has now surmounted that, or perhaps she had any other number of issues. The point is, she has looked at herself, and done much of the work discussed in this book (even if her issues were others, many of the steps in this book apply to all of us), and hence, we might say, she has grown emotionally. She has acquired greater emotional maturity than she had before.

Now she meets someone new. After a dinner date or two, Nina quickly recognizes the *state* or level of emotional maturity of the man (this - the ability to recognize another's state of emotional maturity - is not so hard to do once you begin to 'grow' your own). Perhaps he has not begun work on his own issues, and therefore he may still be needy or emotionally unavailable, or may have any other issues you may care to mention, as most of us do. He may simply not be truly *aware* of them, as so many are not. He might, on the other hand, *also* be a highly intelligent individual, successful in his profession, well-traveled; perhaps he speaks several languages, and has done well financially. Furthermore, he is appears to be a kind and caring person. (In case you think I'm dreaming - that such a person would not *also* have achieved a high level of emotional maturity - let me reassure you that numerous men and women of the calibre I am describing, have walked into my office). So Nina tells herself that there is so much that is good about him that she wants to explore him further. She is also quite attracted to him. Nevertheless, as time goes on, perhaps now they've gone out on a few more dates, and perhaps she's brought some subjects to the table that have more to do with inner work (which she is - due to her own earlier issues - familiar with), and this has allowed her to see that he is truly not interested in looking at himself. She senses, perhaps more than hearing him saying it, that in this regard, he has not evolved. These are matters that at least for now, he is not willing to examine. Regretfully - but with the conviction that this does not bode well for a healthy relationship; after all, she *knows* that telling herself that he will change, or that *she* will be able to change him is probably an exercise in futility - she no longer accepts his invitations. This is a choice based on mis-matched emotional maturity as well as the fact that this negatively impacts the degree of attraction she feels towards the man, despite his many qualities and accomplishments.

And of course it works exactly the same way in the opposite situation. A man who has looked inside and started the process of change and emotional growth, will rarely be attracted to a woman - no matter how accomplished, beautiful, kind, funny, or intelligent, if the level of emotional maturity doesn't fit.

Individuals who are needy and emotionally unavailable are the main focus of this book. The reason they tend to be attracted to each other is precisely because of what I have just described: *they are at a similar level of emotional maturity* (or lack of it), no matter what their outer façade or persona. And until the inner (their emotional maturity) begins reaching for - in this sense - the level of the outer, seeking to attain growth, these individuals will continue to have people who push their buttons or create havoc in their relationship lives. It is only by moving beyond that emotional level, that they are able to have another kind of relationship; we could say: that they are able to *attract* another kind of relationship into their life.

Marbella, September, 2014

Chapter 1

A Closer Look at Emotional Unavailability

Emotional unavailability can be devastating for everyone touched by it.

If you are in a relationship with an emotionally unavailable person, you are probably suffering and asking yourself why it has to be so. You may be telling yourself that you have done everything you could to make the other person happy and yet the other person continues to treat you with coldness or indifference or aloofness. You probably don't understand what you have done to deserve this. There is a strong possibility that you are a person on the needy end of the spectrum of this issue.

If you yourself *are* the emotionally unavailable person, you may feel misunderstood, unloved or mistreated. You may feel that in fact you give a great deal, but that your giving is never appreciated, that far too much is expected of you, and that you are rarely, if ever understood.

People often mistakenly understand emotional unavailability as a ploy on the part of the emotionally unavailable person to *use* others, or to *get without giving*, and while it is true that sometimes that is *exactly* what may happen, it is also true that being emotionally unavailable consistently undermines the existence of the person who suffers from it, and consequently wraps its painful tentacles around those who are in that person's life.

Right here and now I'd like to state that if you are in a relationship with an emotionally unavailable partner, you do not necessarily have the right to consider yourself the victim of such unavailability - as hard as it is - nor do you simply have the right to blame the emotionally unavailable partner for the woes of your relationship.

Equally, if you are in a relationship with a needy partner, please don't believe you necessarily have the right to consider yourself the victim of the needy partner and the way he or she makes you feel pushed to greater commitment than you wish, and suffocated, or intruded upon you in such a way that you feel as though you are never given any space.

Both partners need to own their issues. Neither gets to blame. Understanding the importance of this basic concept is paramount to all that follows in this book.

It's also necessary to understand that emotional unavailability comes in both genders: male and female, and if a person is needy in one relationship, they may be emotionally unavailable in another, because neediness and emotional unavailability are two sides of the same coin. In other words, both individuals have the same issues to deal with, although at first glance what is happening to these people and the things they are doing look as if they are poles apart.

DEFINING THE EMOTIONALLY UNAVAILABLE PERSON

There are several basic aspects to this. These are individuals who are:

- cut off from their own emotions and emotional processes
- cut off from others' emotions and their emotional processes
- very disconnected from the emotional content of their lives
- disengaged from their own sexuality in some fashion
- may appear to be needy at the very beginning of a relationship
- do not know how to love themselves

Let's take a closer look at all of these points.

Cut Off From Their Own Emotional Process

Imagine that a friend or a partner abandons you, either out of the blue, or after an argument, and has now disappeared from your life. Imagine that you feel that you did not deserve such treatment. Clearly, you would experience feelings of hurt, disappointment, pain, sorrow, and so on. You might also feel angry and indignant.

The emotionally unavailable person, however, would not only *not* acknowledge most of these feelings, but would probably say that the whole thing is not really that important, or that it was just as well that it happened. In other words, they would have little recognition of these feelings swirling around inside of them. They might complain of gastric upset, or a headache, or back pain, or knee discomfort, or unexplained difficulties in walking, or any other manifestation that shows that the process went into their body due to it not being acknowledged on the emotional level.

On the other hand, if this person has begun a relationship with someone, and they notice that they are thinking about the other person a lot, and that they enjoy spending time with the other person, and that somehow the sun shines more brightly when they are around the other person, they would not interpret this as the beginning of love, the way many other individuals might, but would perhaps say, after a brief time of enjoying the "warm sunshine" of the other's presence:

- *you're crowding me*
- or *I need more space*
- or *we need to cool it for a while*
- or *I don't know how you do it, but you're really maneuvering yourself into my life*
- or *this is going too quickly for me*
- or simply *I really don't want a relationship*
- or *I always said I didn't want a commitment* (despite the fact that they may often marry or cohabit, but although they may share bed and house, they *rarely share themselves*.)

Clearly, the emotionally unavailable person is saying this *because they are beginning to feel discomfort in the presence of the other person because they are unable to handle the surge of their own emotions in connection to the other person.* This is not conscious, nor is it generally done or said from a position of nastiness or miserliness, even though it may often appear to be that. This is, in actual fact, a defense mechanism, learned, in all likelihood, in childhood, to safeguard the child against hurt from people he/she had loved and who somehow drastically let him down. *Sometimes this letting down happens* only *in the perception of the child.* You will find much more detailed information about this in Chapter 3.

Early childhood attachment studies that look at bonding between the child and its parents or caretaker, indicate that abandonment by the parents, and particularly by the mother, creates much greater problems with later emotional availability than even physical abuse. Abandonment, logically, does not only mean a totally absent parent, but also a parent who disappears for a period of time in the early life of the infant (especially during the first 24 months of life), such as those children whose parents must leave them in hospital, or some kind of institution and are not able to visit frequently. There are also other kinds of abandonment, such as the emotional abandonment of a child, although the parent is physically present. Nevertheless, the experience, whether it truly happened, or was only perceived, or happened for totally innocent reasons (the child's life had to be saved by hospitalizing it) carries enormous weight in the future adult and with his or her relationships with persons of the opposite sex (or the same gender in the case of gay relationships).

Being cut off from their own emotional processes often is described (by these individuals themselves, once they begin to deal with their issue) as not being in their own 'bodies' or 'selves', not being 'grounded', because they notice the difference once they do enter into contact with their own emotional processes.

Next, the emotionally unavailable person is:

Cut Off From Others' Emotional Processes

It follows logically to what we've seen so far that the emotionally unavailable person may not have any insight at all into the state of another person's emotions, *even when faced with that person's tears or recriminations, or pain, which may be totally evident to others, but not necessarily to the emotionally unavailable person.* In the face of these emotions in the other person, the emotionally unavailable person often feels put upon, burdened with an onerous duty, that he or she mainly wants to escape from, because it feels far too heavy, and even often feels dangerous. That makes for a very difficult relationship, to say the least.

Third, emotionally unavailable people are:

Disconnected From the Emotional Content of Their Lives

Despite the disconnection from the emotional content of their lives, emotionally unavailable persons might be very strongly connected to bits of it with those people they do not feel threatened by. For example: they may be very loving and tender to the children – especially the very young children - of other people, or very caring and tender to other people's partners (in the right way, not in the wrong way, i.e. as good and supportive friends). Or they may have a deeply caring relationship with a pet, or be very much into caring for plants, gardening, and so on.

But the connection to their own emotional content is generally non-existent.

I repeat, emotional unavailability tends not to be conscious. It is generally unconscious. The emotionally unavailable person spends an enormous amount of psychological energy maintaining the "wolves at bay". In order to not have to deal with their own emotions, their defense mechanisms have become automatic - a habit, you might say - and spring up, the way a bridge over a castle moat springs up to prevent intruders from approaching too closely.

It is only when this process becomes conscious, that the emotionally unavailable person is in a position to do something about it, and this person may fight tooth and nail in order to *not become aware*. They instinctively know that by becoming aware an inner Pandora's box will open. They may insist that they don't want to leave their comfort zone, or that they never wanted a commitment, and shrug their shoulders and leave it at that, never having come any closer to a conscious realization of their inner scarring and crippled spirit, all the while, *yearning* on some level, for love and acceptance.

The next part of our definition of the emotionally unavailable person concerns their sexuality:

Disengagement From Their Own Sexuality

This is not always the case, but happens often enough to warrant a section in this chapter. Before you disregard this point because your partner has – or you have – if you are the emotionally unavailable person – a strongly sexed nature, please read the remainder of this section carefully.

Sometimes when the emotionally unavailable person has made some outward commitment, such as sharing a home, or having a child with the partner, perhaps deciding to make a new start together in another country, they may withdraw emotionally and sexually, finding it far too emotionally taxing to be engaged on more than one level - in this case, simply living together is enough. Becoming distant from one's partner or not being sexually responsive are also ways of cutting off genuine relating.

So what essentially happens is that there is a strong and passionate sexual relationship before the commitment, whether it's living together, or having a child, or buying a home together or getting married, and then, to the great astonishment and pain of the other partner, sexuality is cut off more and more, with no real explanation. (You will find a far more detailed discussion of this in Chapter 8).

Next, the emotionally unavailable partner:

May Appear to be Needy at the Very Beginning of a Relationship

Although it appears to be a contradiction in terms, the emotionally unavailable partner may appear needy when the new partner first meets him/her. This is apparent due to the number of times - at the beginning - the emotionally unavailable partner may call or otherwise contact the other one, in order to get his/her attention, or in the way the one that later turns out to be emotionally unavailable, makes it clear that what is most important to him - at the beginning - is to spend *all* his free time with the new partner.

This behavior is not necessarily calculating. Rather, I believe it has to do with the tremendous insecurity that lies beneath emotional unavailability, and that - until the new partner is 'securely in hand', creates a *need* that the emotionally unavailable person allows the new partner to see. Only once the new partner has fully fallen into the arms of the other, does the complete specter of emotional unavailability arise.

This, by the way, also explains why, if the needy individual at some point finds a new partner or threatens to leave because he/she is weary of the constant distance and rejection on the partner's side, the emotionally unavailable person once again shows his/her needy side in a frantic attempt to regain the interest of the needy partner, who for the time being is seen as unavailable.

Finally, emotionally unavailable individuals:

Do Not Know How to Love Themselves

Not loving the self, as you will see in later chapters, is one of the most fundamental reasons for unhappiness in our world. A person who *does* love him or herself does not fear being vulnerable, because he *knows* he will be able to take care of himself. Furthermore, loving the self means that a partner will never be taken on because he/she fulfills the role of making you feel good about yourself, because that - feeling good about yourself - will already be part of how you live your life. In other words, you will have learned how to take care of your own needs. Finally, such a person also knows that no matter what happens in his environment (inner or outer), he will be able to take care of himself.

The emotionally unavailable person does not know how to love himself, and hence certainly takes very poor care of himself on emotional and psychological levels, because he has never learned how to do so as a child, and because he believes - in some part of his being - that he is not worthy of love.

The Predator

There may be an element of the predator in such individuals - perhaps more in males who are emotionally unavailable, but certainly I have also seen it in females - and it is generally this characteristic that has given emotionally unavailable people such a bad reputation. Being a predator is seen as something calculating, manipulative, and vile.

And although you may not think of it as such, we could speculate that there is also an element of the predator in the needy person, given that their neediness drives them to find those who might do their bidding, fueled by their neediness. This could also be seen as something calculating, manipulative, and vile.

Nevertheless, as we have seen, neediness and emotional unavailability are two sides of the same coin because both are based on a *lack* of self love, a *fear* of love, and a fear of the hurt that love can engender due to the vulnerability that being in love generally evokes. A person may live out one side of the coin (neediness) in several relationships and then - in a new relationship - may find him or herself living out the other side of the coin (emotional unavailability).

As we will see in Chapter 3, neither of these tend to be deliberate - at least at the beginning - because there is never anything consciously deliberate about the way a defense mechanism arises in childhood.

Chapter 2

A Closer Look at Neediness

Why is it that so often when we feel we are in love, we also feel we are in bondage if anything happens to shake the feeling of "security" in the love? If our partner threatens to leave, or is simply upset or angry with us, many immediately feel a terrible sense of danger. And of course the danger implicit here is that of a need that will no longer be fulfilled, should the partner truly leave. The need will no longer be met. Our inner sense of security - so tenuously based on our need being fulfilled by our partner - is in jeopardy. Is needing part of the love equation? Why does love so often make us dependent on the other person? Shouldn't love be a marvelous and freeing feeling rather than these other sensations of need and fear and dependence? Songs so often say it all:

- Can't Live, if Livin' is Without You
- I Need Your Lovin'
- Ain't No Sunshine When She's Gone
- I Fall to Pieces
- Without You I am Nothing
- I'm Drowning Without Your Love
- If You Leave, I Won't be Able to Breathe

The message each of those songs gives is that when the person you love is no longer with you, you can't go on. You need that person *to be able* to stay alive - at least figuratively speaking. Without the person you love, you are nothing, you can not bear to live.

And while you know that this is not exactly true, many have certainly been in the position of feeling something akin to those words. And it certainly doesn't help that we have all been bombarded with such lyrics since we were too young to even understand what they entailed.

So what does it mean? Does it really mean that loving someone implies that you need the other person so much that you simply feel you can not go on without them? Or could all that be a fallacy?

Let's examine what happens in a typical *love* scenario. Boy meets girl (man meets woman), chemistry, infatuation, bliss, love, we've all been there and know how that part of it goes. But what is *really* happening? Raging hormones answer only a small part of the question, even though they can create a vast impact. University of Pisa's Donatella Marazziti's work on romantic love activating parts of the brain associated with addiction has found that falling in love is a bit like going crazy from the point of view of brain chemicals and hormones.

Carl Gustav Jung said that our psyche is so infinitely intelligent that it *attracts* us to certain individuals (as certain individuals' psyche causes them to be attracted to us) in order that we *experience precisely that which we need to grow*. And as I wrote at the beginning of this book: in our emotional lives we tend to attract to us - and have relationships with - people who have attained (or stagnated at) the *same* level of emotional maturity as we have.

So how do we typically grow? By going through an experience of some sort that may not be easy. We grow at school by learning, studying, and taking exams. We grow in life by becoming more aware, and we generally tend to become more aware when some life experience obliges us to do so.

By extrapolating, we might say that in relationships we grow most quickly through experiences that are not necessarily easy. And going back to Jung, he clearly proposes that throughout the course of our lives it is our psyche that in its infinite intelligence leads us to be attracted to *precisely* those individuals who most have the potential to be instruments in our individual growth. In order for that to work, evidently we first have to be fully *in relationship* with those people. So we fall in love, we begin to feel that our happiness depends in some measure on the other person, and so begins our *need* of that person.

An external need, in others words, when we depend on something *external* to ourselves for our well-being, frequently carries within it the seeds for failure. In the case of a relationship, it may often be the cause of power plays between the two people, the less *needy* one being the one to dominate the relationship, and the *needier* one to resentfully accept this dominance due to his or her need for the other partner (also see Chapters 12 and 13).

So what causes us to believe that we love because we need? Is there anything mature and adult about that kind of sentiment? Where else can it lead us other than at first to dependency, and later to - eventual - frustration and pain? And don't forget: if the other person is also on the same page and loves you because of how you fill *their* needs, then they will go through a similar process. And sooner or later you are going to let them down – as they do you – because it is very difficult to be *responsible for another's well-being by fulfilling their needs*, the needs that they should be fulfilling themselves.

So to fall in love and go through this process is excellent. Because the place we come out at the other end of the tunnel is indeed worth its weight in gold. *To love without needing* is the priceless gift we can receive from having fallen in love and having chosen to use the challenges it evokes to further our growth, rather than to take the simple way out and blame the other for now no longer fulfilling our needs, or no longer making us happy. To love without needing is the priceless gift we can receive because we fell in love.

But of course at this point, for the individual who suffers from chronic neediness, this is not yet a goal he or she has managed to reach, or even *wants* to reach.

Love is such a vast part of life, whether because - ideally - it brings sheer joy such as almost nothing else is capable of doing, or because ultimately it may lead to agonizing suffering. More often than not it is a harbinger of a bit of both. So if I were to ask if you are "in love", or if you "love", since one appears to automatically imply the other, you might find my question quite absurd. Or could it be the case that being 'in love' does not necessarily imply 'loving'?

Being in love brings to mind that heart-pounding, mind-jolting passion we feel when the person we say we are in love with enters the room, touches us, or unexpectedly smiles or looks at us. It refers to the moments when we feel most alive, when we can not imagine what life would be like without the other, when we most fear being abandoned by the other, when we are capable of surviving on two hours of sleep, need little food, and no matter what else occurs in our existence, we gaze benignly on life, because we are in love. The sun shines brilliantly in an impossibly azure-blue sky, even in fog, wind, rain, and storms. We pity ordinary mortals who do not share in our sublime experience, and in the rosy haze of our over-powering state of being in love we fail to see those small or large shortcomings in the beloved that are clearly and utterly obvious to others simply because we are in love. Being in love – and being lucky enough to be reciprocated in that feeling - is nearly unequalled by any other experience in life.

Loving, on the other hand, rarely goes about doing so by wearing rose-colored spectacles. Loving may have seen its beginnings with the less conscious state of being in love, but loving implies – you guessed it – consciousness and awareness of the reality of the other. That, in turn, implies being very aware of yourself, your thoughts, feelings, actions, and reactions. And this self awareness implies an individual who strives to take total responsibility for him or herself, who is not with another person because he or she *needs* the other person, but because the two people, by loving one another, *complement* one another from a position of individual freedom and strength. *Loving* is a state of affairs that is as different from *being in love* as day is to night. Loving, if it really *is* loving, is so much more awe-inspiring and endlessly magnificent than being in love.

Defining the Needy Person

There are four basic aspects to this. These are individuals who:

- believe they are in close contact to their emotions, when, in fact, the opposite is true
- depend on the object of their love for their most essential well-being
- have not learned to take care of and love themselves
- have unhealthy boundaries and may be very manipulative in order to obtain what they need from their partner

- may frequently appear to be independent individuals as long as they are not in a relationship

Let's take a closer look at these points.

Believe They Have a Close Connection to Their Emotions, When in Fact, the Opposite is True

Although you might not think so at first glance, and certainly, if you were to ask one of them they would not agree, needy people are closely related on the psycho-emotional level, to the emotionally unavailable individual. *That is why* - in a nutshell - *these two issues form part of the same coin.*

The lack of close connection to their own emotions can clearly be seen in the following example from my case files.

Lily (not her real name) had been in needy relationships throughout her adult life. When she came to see me along with her emotionally unavailable husband Andrew, she told me that what she most desired in the whole world was a close emotional relationship with her partner, and yet in each of her principle relationships, this had been denied to her due to - according to her - the emotional unavailability of these men. Andrew concurred that he did indeed have issues expressing and feeling emotions, but told me he wanted to work on this aspect of his heart and psyche, and buckled down. He began to practice in some of the ways you will find in this book, and brought himself to a place where he wanted a connection with Lily that was not what he had shared with her to that point. In other words, he wanted a true emotional connection.

You might imagine that we now had the perfect solution to their marriage. He wanted what Lily wanted, and had worked enough on himself in order to apply it to their relationship.

What happened next was a surprise to Andrew. With the inner work in which he had been engaging - and as you will come to realize as you continue reading - what had changed was how aware he was of himself when feeling 'threatened' by closeness, how much responsibility he assumed for himself, his thoughts, feelings, and reactions, and therefore how he communicated with Liily had changed as well. When she craved emotional closeness he was willing to move in her direction, but he equally demanded of her that she become more aware of *her*self, in order that her neediness would have a chance to evolve to greater independence. He wanted her to recognize that her well-being and happiness did not depend on him, but on her. She initially took this to mean that he was once again making himself unavailable, or not wishing to engage with her, but when he explained that what it really meant - if she were to take on that task - was that they would be able to communicate emotionally on levels they had never dreamed of, she shied back.

In other words, by Andrew asking Lily to move - at her own pace - from neediness to healthy independence, all *her* fears about vulnerability and *adult* emotions rose to the surface. Being needy had been her way of avoiding real emotional connection. In some fashion it meant that another person (her partner) was responsible for her emotional life, and if she was not happy, she could blame the responsible party (in this case, the emotionally unavailable partner) for that. To now release this defense mechanism was not something she was prepared to do. Her fears were too high. After some time, with Andrew now growing to be more and more emotionally *available* every day, but Lily remaining needy and mired in her own fear of - in this case - emotional maturity - they divorced.

As you can see, the fears of taking on responsibility for one's own emotional life and for one's vulnerability by so doing, can be daunting not only to the emotionally unavailable partner, but *also* to the needy one.

Secondly, needy individuals:

Depend on the Object of Their Love for Their Most Essential Well-being

They may feel good or bad depending on the state of their relationship to the object of their love. If the partner (even if this is still a very new, unproven, and tenuous relationship situation) is being perceived by the needy person as being uninterested in them (even if only for a few hours, potentially due to work having been brought home, or perhaps a family situation - on the part of the partner - that requires time and attention), distant, rejecting, or involved in something - anything - *other* than in the needs, and desires, and in shoring up the insecurities of the needy partner, then the needy partner will generally decline in psycho-emotional well-being. And of course there will not be the slightest doubt in the needy partner's mind that this is due to - and the fault of - the object of their love. They *depend* on the partner's attention to feel well.

They may feel good or bad depending on whether they perceive the object of their love to be in a good mood. If the partner - and again, this can happen even if the relationship is still very new - is worried, stressed, or preoccupied, or any variation thereof, or simply in a bad mood, the needy person will invariably take this to mean that the way the partner feels is connected directly to him/her and hence that it *reflects negatively* on the state and health of their relationship. If the subject is discussed, and the other partner clearly affirms that his/her state of mind has nothing at all to do with the needy partner, but rather, with work-related or other issues not connected to the needy partner, the latter will generally not believe it, and will not feel good - which we might rephrase as *secure* - until the partner's frame of mind or mood has been re-established at which point the needy partner is able to breathe a sigh of relief.

None of this tends to fall within the *aware* aspect of the needy partner's psyche - and most often it is also not understood consciously by the unavailable partner; rather, he or she may simply take it to mean - again - how smothering the needy partner is.

They may feel good or bad depending on how much face time and contact they have with the object of their love on any given day. This derives from the fact that a needy person will generally want a greater than normal amount of time with the new partner, but even when the partner is no longer new, the situation continues along similar lines. And so the result is a very insistent and strident demand for a great deal of face time, phone calls, text messages, etc., as opposed to someone in a healthier relationship who simply does not need this amount of reassurance. This is also the reason needy persons such as the ones I have described, tend to rapidly lose interest in their friends and hobbies or other outside interests, once a new relationship appears in their life, and they dedicate themselves to it in this wholehearted fashion. However - as said - they do it to feed their neediness, so it is anything but healthy.

Third, needy individuals:

Have Not Learned to Take Care of & Love Themselves

This is implicit in the above points. A person who loves him or herself would never be dependent on the moods or negative emotions of another to feel good about him or herself. Such a person would recognize that those moods or emotions are separate from him/her, and hence know that they say nothing about the health of the relationship. They might even be psychologically and emotionally aware enough to understand that moods tend to indicate a lack of self-awareness on the part of the moody partner. A person who loves and takes good care of himself will check his own emotions or mood when the partner is in such a place, and will do whatever is necessary in order to maintain an inner state of harmony, *even* when the emotions of the partner are caused by important and verifiable reasons.

Not loving the self, just as with the emotionally unavailable individual, comes from never having learned how to do so as a child, and from a deep-rooted belief that there is nothing essentially lovable, worthy, or good about the self. This belief undermines the very existence and well-being of such people.

Fourth, needy individuals:

Have Unhealthy Boundaries & May Be Very Manipulative

The fact that the majority of needy individuals have poor boundaries makes sense in view of all the points discussed thus far. A needy person will do whatever is necessary to ensure the smooth continuation of receiving all that he/she *needs* from the partner in order to feel good, as well as safe. Therefore if the partner is inappropriate in some way, or behaves in an unacceptable fashion, the needy partner rarely speaks up. It may be that after a period of repeated unacceptable behavior (typical examples include shouting or being verbally aggressive, being unfaithful, coming home and simply not engaging in any meaningful way, belittling and denigrating the needy partner, not taking on any responsibility for household chores, etc.), the needy partner explodes, shouting, crying, accusing, or even threatening to leave, most frequently occasioning a tapering off of unacceptable behavior on the part of the partner - for a time - perhaps even abject apologies in order that things return to the status quo, and then the cycle typically begins again.

When poor boundaries and a lack of self-love are not tackled in a conscious and self-responsible fashion, as discussed elsewhere in this book, little will change to cause the relationship to become healthier.

The manipulative aspect of the needy partner may appear in a variety of ways, ranging from moods, or crying, and tantrums all the way to threatening to harm him or herself or to commit suicide. Being a victim is another favorite. Clearly, compassion is needed for a person who feels such tactics are required, and needs help with respect to better understanding the self and the motivations for such behavior.

Finally, needy individuals:

May Frequently Appear to be Independent Individuals as Long as They are not in a Relationship

When you meet a needy partner for the first time, you may find that their behavior is very independent. They have work, outside interests, hobbies, sports activities, charitable work, and so on, and of course, they have a circle of friends.

This lulls many an unsuspecting partner - perhaps one who has had relationships with needy individuals before, into believing that this new partner is not needy in the least, because the neediness does not appear until shortly after the beginning of the relationship. The simple reason is this: until the needy partner falls in love, his/her *neediness button* has not yet been pushed. It's the state of being in love that changes how they behave. You will find further information about this in Chapters 12, 13, and 14.

Chapter 3

Some Origins

Before I even begin to discuss how emotional unavailability and neediness originate, I need to reiterate the fact that in the majority of cases nothing about these issues tends to be deliberate. There is never anything consciously deliberate about the way a defense mechanism arises in childhood, and this is what the two sides of this particular coin represent. A case in point: a man who refuses to commit should not blithely be judged as being manipulative or callous, a philanderer, or heartless being, although *on the surface* he may very well appear to be so.

Furthermore, the older he gets, the more of a history of this nature he acquires, and hence the more those who sit in judgement reach the conclusion that they are right. The same could, of course, be said about the emotionally unavailable woman. Another case in point: a woman whose neediness appears emotionally manipulative (of her partner, parents, children, or friends) to a high degree, does not generally behave in such a manner in a deliberate fashion. And again, the same could be said about the needy man.

It is true, however, that some individuals who have become habituated to using these defense mechanisms over the course of many years, have clearly observed their effect on others, and so the emotionally unavailable man may have noticed that this behavior *magically* draws a certain kind of woman to him. Likewise, the needy woman will have observed that certain individuals always seem to do her bidding if she expresses her neediness in emotionally manipulative ways (and the same applies to both genders when their issue is expressed in the converse fashion of what I have just stated).

At this point, of course, we could conclude that the two mechanisms: emotional unavailability and neediness are being deliberately and calculatingly used in order to manipulate another human being, and due to this behavior therefore, there is an element of truth in that conclusion. Nevertheless, in my experience and in my opinion, this is never fully the case, *until the person involved is fully conscious of not only what caused him/her to become like this, but also conscious of how the defense mechanism is implemented time after time due to fear.* The fact is that until all of this is made conscious, the fear is generally not recognized as such. Rather, as with any number of other psychological, emotional, or physical issues, it means that when such a person *uses* the manipulative actions deliberately, while we might argue that they are selfish or inconsiderate, I would nevertheless defend them to a